Original title:
The Orchard's Joy

Copyright © 2025 Creative Arts Management OÜ
All rights reserved.

Author: Maya Livingston
ISBN HARDBACK: 978-1-80586-351-9
ISBN PAPERBACK: 978-1-80586-823-1

The Heartbeat of Nature

In the garden where laughter blooms,
Squirrels dance in their fuzzy costumes.
Trees whisper secrets, oh what a sight,
While bees take selfies in the sunlight.

A flower's hat is quite the craze,
Each petal struts in a frilly blaze.
The bumblebees buzz a rollicking song,
As worms wiggle along, oh so strong!

Boughs Heavy with Promise

Apples are juggling on branches tall,
While pears are plotting a fruit-salad brawl.
Even the cherries are bursting with cheer,
Offering smiles, oh, don't get too near!

The branches sway like a limber dance,
While nutty chipmunks take every chance.
They'll snatch a treat and dart into shade,
Laughing and giggling, all mischief displayed!

Petals and Playfulness

In the meadows, petals throw a feast,
Where butterflies twirl, from west to east.
A dandelion dreams of a fluffball fight,
While crickets chirp tunes, oh so light!

The sunbeams wink at the buzzing crowd,
As ladybugs lounge, feeling quite proud.
Grasshoppers hop with a comedic flair,
In this vibrant world, laughter's everywhere!

Sun-Kissed Dreams

The sun dips low, painting skies—a show,
While shadows stretch like a big hello.
Fireflies twinkle with a wink and glow,
Dancing around like they're stealing the show!

The evening breeze has a cheeky tease,
Tickling the daisies with playful ease.
Stars come out, joining the spree,
In this wild, joyful jamboree!

A Symphony of Ripeness

In a tree, a peach is laughing loud,
The apple joined, it feels so proud.
The cherries giggle, what a sight,
While plums strike poses in the light.

The pears tell jokes that make you snort,
And lemons dance with a wild cavort.
Each fruit a player in the show,
As bees buzz along, stealing the flow.

Nature's Gentle Lullaby

The berries snore as the sun peeks high,
While grapes get tangled, oh my, oh my!
An orange rolls, slips on a peel,
And all the fruits share a hearty meal.

The raspberries whisper sweet little dreams,
Of flowing rivers and sparkling streams.
Bananas chuckle, their stories grand,
As motley friends form a fruit band.

The Quiet Festivities

A party's brewing under the leaves,
With tiny ants wearing fruit-shaped sleeves.
Kiwi struts with a feathered crown,
While cucumbers giggle, never a frown.

The quiet laughs echo in the sun,
Fruit salads cheer, all having fun.
Lime farts jokes that make fruit burst,
This silent joy is truly the first!

Savoring Each Moment

On a branch, the apples start a race,
With juicy lemons joining the chase.
Grapefruit slides, giving berry a shove,
While fig blinks and gets ready to shove.

The sun dips low, laughs fill the air,
Watermelons roll without a care.
They all break free from the mundane,
Savoring laughter, no sign of shame.

Whispers of the Wild

In fields where apples bounce and roll,
Squirrels wear hats, a goofy goal.
They tease the pears, all plump and bright,
While grapes giggle under sunlight.

A rabbit hops with a jolly glee,
Sipping dew from a tiny spree.
The cherries start a dance so sweet,
While lemons tumble off their seat.

A plump tomato tells a joke,
While prancing beets nearly choke.
The berries blush in fruity cheer,
As laughter ripples far and near.

With laughter spreading like the bloom,
Each fruit finds joy in nature's room.
Together they giggle, sing, and play,
In this wild, funny cabaret!

Nurtured by Nature

Bananas don hats, quite the sight,
They wave at the sun, feeling bright.
Lemons roll down the grassy hill,
With oranges lining up for the thrill.

A clever peach struts with flair,
While berries giggle, light as air.
They play hide and seek in the vine,
As melons swing and toe the line.

The carrots wear shades, looking fine,
While pumpkins juggle in a line.
A splash of joy in the morning dew,
With every laugh, the day feels new.

In this silly plot, all fruits convey,
The fun of life in a bright bouquet.
Together they laugh, dance, and tease,
In nature's arms, with the freshest breeze.

Embracing the Season

Fruits dangle like chandeliers,
Waiting for pickers and cheers.
Squirrels dance, they're on a spree,
While I trip over a bramble tree.

Sunshine tickles the apples' skin,
While bees buzz, trying to blend in.
A watermelon's gone on a roll,
And I'm just losing my control!

Lemonade spills, laughter erupts,
Giggling while the fruit stew erupts.
Oh, the mishaps, a silly parade,
Making memories like lemonade.

Every Tree Tells a Story

Under branches, secrets hide,
Like a squirrel with its loot inside.
One tree says, 'Watch out for the ants!',
While the peach tree whispers, 'Do the dance!'

A cherry claims it saw a bird,
Making funny sounds, but so absurd.
The fig tree grins with a cheeky wink,
As I ponder if they all can think.

Oranges argue which one's the best,
While pears just lounge, enjoying the rest.
Each morning brings a new tall tale,
In this grove, laughter cannot fail.

Fruits of Laughter

Grapes are giggling on the vine,
Jokes are ripe, and so divine.
Oh, the plums play practical pranks,
While apples join in, giving thanks!

Bananas slip, a comic show,
As peaches blush with a fabulous glow.
Watermelons sing silly songs,
While jiving with ants and laughing throngs.

Every fruit shares its funny charm,
Creating chaos without alarm.
Laughter echoes through every tree,
In this realm where joy runs free.

Whispers in the Trees

The trees gossip, oh what a sight,
With branches swaying in pure delight.
"Did you hear about the pear's new hat?"
"Is it true the kiwi tried to chat?"

A breeze carries jokes through the leaves,
As oranges tease the grapes for their sleeves.
The apples plot a clever scheme,
Wishing to steal the peaches' dream.

Berry bushes chuckle and sway,
While nuts shout out, "We're here to play!"
In this whimsical, green retreat,
Every whisper brings joy bittersweet.

Sun-Drenched Symphony

In the sun, the fruit hangs low,
A squirrel steals an apple, oh no!
With every bounce, he tries to flee,
While birds above sing, "Look at me!"

Breezes dance with lazy glee,
Lemons swirl in perfect spree.
The cherries giggle, round and sweet,
While bees buzz by, tapping their feet.

As laughter spills beneath the trees,
I trip on roots and land with ease.
Grass stains my pants; I start to pout,
The fruits all laugh, "You'll grow out!"

With jests and juice, all is bright,
Each moment blessed, pure delight.
Who knew the orchard held such fun?
Next week, I'll bring a friend for run!

Harmonics of Harmony

Under branches, music flows,
A cat plays piano with her toes.
Cherries eavesdrop on a tune,
While raccoons poke heads up at noon.

A pumpkin rolled to join the band,
With fluffy bunnies lending a hand.
Peaches hum, the apples sway,
What a show, come watch, they say!

A dapper goose, with bowtie neat,
Dances fancy on webbed feet.
He waltzes round the wise old tree,
Chasing shadows, wild and free.

As night descends, the show must stop,
The stars join in, no need to swap.
Make sure to come next week, my friend,
Our orchard never sees the end!

Threads of Delight

In the grove, the stitches laugh,
A squirrel knits a fruit scarf!
With glee, he twirls his yarn so bright,
While turtles join to share a bite.

A weaver bird sings notes so fine,
"Grab a peach, it's snack time divine!"
Bananas slip, and oh, what a fall,
As giggles burst from one and all!

An old frog croaks a funky beat,
Riding the rhythm with tiny feet.
Grasshoppers hop with grace and sound,
As laughter weaves all around.

When dusk arrives, they take a bow,
The night awaits; it's time, somehow.
With dreams of stitches left to play,
I shall return, come what may!

Vibrant Undertones

Under leaves, the colors clash,
A raccoon sneaks for one big snack.
He trips on roots, but don't you fret,
A friendly beetle calls him "pet!"

A cantaloupe joins, rolling round,
"You'll never catch me!" is its sound.
While berries clash in berry brawl,
Laughter echoes through the hall.

The sun dips low, and shadows play,
Dancing figures mark the day.
With silly pranks and fruit parade,
In this grove, we're all just made!

Let's gather 'round, we'll share our cheer,
In colors bright, we'll hold it dear.
With every giggle, every jest,
This patch of joy is simply the best!

Harvest of Happiness

In the field where laughter grows,
The apples dance, striking poses.
A squirrel juggles, what a sight,
While bees hum tunes from left to right.

Cherries giggle, plump and round,
As farmers trip upon the ground.
With baskets full, they shout hooray,
It's just another harvest day!

Pumpkins roll in playful cheer,
While crows peek in, they've come near.
They steal a pie, then flap away,
Oh, harvest thievery at play!

In the sun, with fruit galore,
We laugh until our sides are sore.
So raise a glass of cider sweet,
To laughter shared and tasty treat!

Beneath the Boughs

Beneath the boughs of fruit so bright,
A raccoon dreams of endless night.
With snacks galore, he's in a trance,
While apples roll and squirrels prance.

Dancing pears hold silly contests,
As chopstick wielding kids take rests.
They swing and miss, both take a tumble,
While giggles burst, and fruit wheels rumble.

A goat arrives, declaring pride,
He munches leaves, a tasty guide.
He butts a tree, it shakes with mirth,
And fruit falls down; oh, joyful girth!

Beneath the boughs, we sip and share,
Nuts and fruit, we haven't a care.
With each bite and laugh in ease,
Life's silly moments come to tease!

Sweet Serenity

In the garden of sweet delight,
Strawberries giggle, oh what a sight!
They tease the bees with fragrant air,
While giggles echo everywhere!

Lemonade flows in jugs so wide,
While ants march by, their wonky stride.
They dance on blueberry hills galore,
As friends munch down, forevermore!

A watermelon spills, it's quite a scene,
With juice that splatters, oh, how obscene!
The seeds launch out like little darts,
While laughter grows, it fills our hearts.

Sweet serenity, a joyful mess,
With fruity battles, who could guess?
We toast again, with smiles so wide,
In this sweet place, where laughs abide!

Blossoms in the Breeze

Blossoms flutter in the air,
As I trip over, unaware.
A butterfly lands on my nose,
Its laughter tickles, goodness knows!

But down the lane, there's cider bold,
Giggling fruits, they never get old.
Apples wink; they're up to tricks,
While nuts roll by, oh what a mix!

A parrot squawks, "Who stole my pie?"
As we all giggle, oh me, oh my!
With laughter ringing through the trees,
We chase the fruit on summer's breeze.

Beneath the sky, with friends so dear,
We sip and munch, without a fear.
So let the blossoms swirl and play,
In our funny orchard getaway!

Life Among the Blossoms

In a field of blooms so bright,
Bees buzzed and danced with delight,
A squirrel stole a peachy treat,
While birds chirped in a funny beat.

The flowers giggled in the breeze,
As pollen tickled buzzing knees,
A rabbit pondered with a frown,
Why carrots don't grow in this town.

A butterfly on a flower bed,
Laughed at onions, 'You smell like dread!'
While worms wriggled, plotting a game,
Of hopscotch, but their fame stayed tame.

Then came a cat, adorned in style,
Stretched out, she yawned with a smile,
As fruit flew high in playful jest,
In this blooming place, we felt blessed.

Whimsy in the Orchard

Underneath a sunny glow,
Bouncing bunnies put on a show,
With floppy ears and silly hops,
They tangled in the apple crops.

A crow wore shades, looking so cool,
While mushrooms danced, breaking the rule,
They twirled in circles, round and round,
Trying hard not to fall down.

An old tree moaned with a creak,
Saying, 'Kids, it's time to sneak,
And find those apples, red and round,
Just make sure laughter's the only sound!'

The breeze swayed like a jovial wave,
Tickling cheeks, oh how it gave,
Each branch blossomed with joy anew,
Creating scenes that made us woo.

Sun-Kissed Visions

Sunshine gleamed on golden fruit,
A plump pear danced in a cute suit,
It rolled down hills, a merry sight,
Chasing shadows in pure delight.

A pig in shades, what a charmer,
Sipped lemonade with much glamour,
While apples giggled overhead,
'Oh, the things we could've said!'

Juggling cherries, all in a row,
Made a mess, but stole the show,
Duck waddled in, quacking a tune,
Setting the stage for a silly swoon.

Daisies whispered with a grin,
'Who knew chaos could feel like kin?'
With laughter echoing through the air,
Sun-kissed days took away our care.

Fertile Imagination

In a patch where all is ripe,
Frogs strummed tunes on a grape pipe,
While ants debated who's the best,
At building homes—a busy quest.

A prune contested an apricot,
On who could juggle a lemon dot,
With silly faces and playful cheers,
As laughter drowned out all our fears.

A wandering goat, with a crown,
Claimed the title of the best clown,
And apples rolled, giving a shout,
'Come join the fun, don't sit out!'

Under a sky, so crisp and wide,
We chased our dreams with joyful pride,
Imagining life, both wild and free,
In a world where humor is key.

Fruits of Serenity

In the garden, fruits do dance,
Laughing peaches take a chance.
Apples giggle, pears run fast,
Chasing shadows, having a blast.

Bananas slip with joyful yells,
While oranges sing their citrus spells.
Plums tell jokes in pastried hue,
Berries join in, oh what a brew!

Lemons toss their zesty zest,
Making all the fruits feel blessed.
With every chuckle, roots grow deep,
In this laughter, joy we keep.

So grab a bite, come share the cheer,
In this fruity world, we live dear.
Where smiles blossom, oh so wide,
And nature's winks can't be denied.

Whispers in Sunlight

Underneath the golden glow,
Tomatoes gossip, putting on a show.
Carrots jump in place so spry,
As radishes grin, oh my, oh my!

The daisies wink, the cucumbers tease,
Pineapples dance with a sizzling breeze.
Pumpkins prance in patchy rows,
Spreading laughter from their toes.

Cabbages play hide and seek,
While the sunflowers peek, oh so meek.
In this patch, so full of life,
Every laugh cuts through the strife.

So let the sunlight lift your heart,
Join the dance, and take your part.
In this garden, full of cheer,
Whispers of joy are always near.

Harvesting Laughter

With baskets full, we gather round,
A medley of giggles is what we've found.
Watermelons roll with a playful cheer,
While cantaloupes chuckle, "Come over here!"

Radishes tell tales of their sprouty might,
While broccoli bursts with laughter, quite bright.
Chestnuts join in, cracking their jokes,
And figs just snicker as humor invokes.

Peas in pods giggle in pairs,
A chorus of laughter fills the air.
As we gather goodies for supper tonight,
These veggies' antics are pure delight.

So join the fun, and don't miss out,
In this harvest, we laugh and shout.
With every bite, let joy ignite,
In this colorful feast, everything feels right.

Blossoms of Delight

In colors bright, the flowers joke,
Tulips tease with a playful poke.
Daisies giggle, roses blush,
In a garden party, there's no rush.

Bumblebees buzz like a stand-up crew,
Sharing puns that are sweet and true.
Lilies laugh till their petals sway,
As daisies hum, "Let's dance and play!"

Every bloom tells a funny tale,
Bringing laughter with every gale.
Nature's jokes lift spirits so light,
In this flowered realm, everything's right.

So sip some nectar, join the fun,
In this garden, we've all just begun.
With every blossom, joy takes flight,
A riot of laughter, pure delight.

Lush Discoveries

In a grove where laughter spills,
Fruits bounce like they have wills.
Apples giggle, pears do wink,
Bananas dance, oh what a link!

Bees buzz by with comic flair,
Chasing shadows, light as air.
A squirrel juggles, what a sight,
Nutty antics day and night!

Fog rolls in with a grin,
Muffled whispers of their sin.
A secret pact, they all agree,
Fruit's a feast for you and me!

So in this patch of pure delight,
Join the fun, get fruits in sight!
With every bite, a chuckle blooms,
In this jungle of sweet perfumes.

Sunshine through Leaves

Sunshine peeks through leafy hats,
Tickling fruits as they chat.
Citrus jokes, oh what a zest,
Together they all feel the best!

Lemon-lime in a playful tease,
Joking well with fluttering bees.
Oranges laugh till they turn red,
"Don't let the grape go to your head!"

With each drip of golden light,
They sway and shimmy, feeling bright.
Cherries giggle, "Let's be bold!"
In a fruit bowl, the tales unfold!

Grappling leaves in a silly fight,
Who will wear the sun so right?
In this canopy of cheer and flair,
Each fruit's a star in the sunny air!

Awakening Fulfillment

Morning breaks with a sly grin,
Ripening dreams begin to spin.
Peaches blush, they've hit the stage,
Dancing freely, there's no cage!

Berries burst with a syrupy laugh,
Sipping dew like it's a craft.
Melon smiles wide, it's a feast,
Inviting all for a fruity beast.

Figs in hats, all posh and neat,
Throw a picnic, it's hard to beat!
Gather round and share a slice,
Fruit's a morsel, oh so nice!

Twinkling lights from above the green,
The best of times we've ever seen!
In this lively, joyful spread,
Let's get fruity, go ahead!

Rejoicing in Ripeness

Beneath the boughs, with laughs we wander,
Ripe delights make hearts grow fonder.
But wait, what's that? A sneaky crow,
Attempting to put on quite a show!

Watermelons roll with glee,
While oranges fall, "Catch me, whee!"
Grapes all join, a cheerful crowd,
Who said fruit is not allowed?

Avocado wears a charming hat,
"The ripening game's where it's at!"
Every fruit in sync and rhyme,
Laughing loud, it's fruiting time!

With jelly beans in fruity jars,
We're dancing like we're little stars.
In this patch of endless cheer,
Rejoice with all, the time is here!

Savoring Sweetness

Beneath the tree limbs, we play all day,
Chasing the berries that roll away.
With cheeks full of laughter, we munch and we feast,
Sticky fingers and giggles, oh, what a beast!

Fruit flies are swarming, we swat and we shout,
While squirrels are plotting their next little route.
"Hey, that's my apple!" we screech in delight,
But they're gone in a flash, what a comical sight!

Juicy delights hang just out of our reach,
With antics resembling a slapstick speech.
We climb and we tumble, but hey, what a spree!
Just blame it on gravity—it's never on me!

Now, with bellies full, we lay on the ground,
Extremely content, oh, laughter abound.
The sun sets above, a glorious show,
As we soak in the sweetness, with joy in tow.

Underneath the Foliage

Beneath the green canopy, secrets reside,
We hide from our chores, what a curious slide!
With laughter and whispers, we craft our own play,
As shadows and sunlight dance in dismay.

The ants are our troops, so serious and bold,
While crickets serenade with stories of old.
We wage tiny battles on terrain of grass,
While the world overhead simply watches and laughs.

Fragrant aromas of sweetness do waft,
Yet every heist met with too much heft!
We giggle and stumble, like leaves in a breeze,
As mother hens cluck, "Now, don't scrape your knees!"

With laughter that tickles our bellies like fruit,
We take sips of sunshine, and dance in our loot.
For here in this haven, we find our own peace,
Beneath the green foliage, our laughter won't cease.

Glorious Growth

Tiny seeds planted, oh what a surprise,
With whims of the wind, they reach for the skies.
Watch! Here's a sprout! It's a green wiggle fest,
Not quite what we expected, but let's give it rest!

As petals unfold, and buds take their stance,
We're waiting for fruit, just a slip and a chance.
With watering cans, we dance in the sun,
Pretending this garden is all just for fun.

Giggles erupt at each tumble and fall,
The veggies don't mind, they grow big and tall.
Then came the day when the first fruit appeared,
We cheered and we shouted, "We've actually steered!"

Yet the strawberries squish when we give them a squeeze,

While cucumbers grow, still lacking some ease.
"So, nature's a joker!" we laugh through the pain,
For glorious growth keeps us dancing in rain.

Nectar of Nostalgia

Under the fruit boughs, old stories delight,
Of summer enchantments and dappled twilight.
Sipping on sweetness like candy from trees,
With memories popping like bubbles in breeze.

"Remember that time?" with a wink and a grin,
We ventured to pick, but came back with a spin!
In baskets of laughter, we gathered our prize,
Only to find an odd-vegetable surprise!

Peaches like pillows, while plums roll away,
Did they plan it together? Oh, let's just say,
The nectar of nostalgia is mixed with a laugh,
And trees know the stories, they stand as our staff!

As dusk starts to settle, we cherish the day,
With friends by our side, we sing and we play.
So here's to the memories and fruits that we take,
For laughter is sweeter, make no mistake!

A Symphony of Growth

In the garden, veggies dance,
Tomatoes twirl, they take a chance.
Carrots giggle, roots entwine,
Lettuce sings, 'This salad's fine!'

Bees are buzzing, quite the crew,
Wearing hats, oh what a view!
With flowers swaying, petals bright,
Nature's party, pure delight!

Rabbits hop, they're feeling bold,
Stealing carrots, that's their gold.
While squirrels plot their nutty schemes,
In this garden, all's a dream!

So grab a fork and take a bite,
Joy's in the crunch, oh what a sight!
With every munch, a giggle flies,
In this patch, happiness lies!

Colors of Celebration

Fruit loops hang from every branch,
Mangoes bob, let's have a dance!
Pineapples wear their golden crowns,
Oranges roll, avoiding frowns.

Berries gossip in the sun,
'Life's too sweet; let's have some fun!'
Watermelons burst with delight,
Juicy laughter, pure delight.

Peaches waltz in cozy rows,
Bananas slide, slipping like pros.
Each colorful smile, a tasty treat,
Nature's feast, can't be beat!

So let's toast with fruit in hand,
Come join this zany fruitland!
With every bite and cheerful cheer,
We celebrate, it's time to steer!

Harvest Moonlight

Under the stars, the pumpkins grin,
Trick-or-treaters planning their win.
In the moonlight, apples glow,
Caramel dreams begin to flow.

Goblins sneak with candy bags,
In the field, they hide like rags.
Ghostly whispers, too much fun,
Harvest time has now begun!

The corn maze twists, a silly chase,
Laughter echoes in this place.
With hayrides rolling through the night,
Every bump brings pure delight!

So raise your mugs of apple juice,
To magic nights and festive ruse.
In moonlit fields, we all unite,
Harvest joy shines ever bright!

Fruitful Fantasies

In the land where berries grow,
There's a tree that loves to show.
With jelly beans hanging low,
It's a sight, a wacky show!

Grapes are gossiping like friends,
'Where's the party? Let's make amends!'
Kiwi whispers tales so sweet,
In this orchard, fun's a treat.

Peaches prank, they stain your shirt,
Pomegranates throw a little dirt.
Cherries giggle, laughter rings,
In the branches, joy just springs!

So dance among the fruity cheer,
Join the jive, let's all be near.
In this play, we find our fate,
Munching joy, oh it's so great!

Tales from the Canopy

In trees so tall, the fruit hangs low,
Squirrels dance, putting on a show.
They swat at bees like little champs,
As apples tumble in crazy stamps.

The pears giggle, all round and sweet,
As rabbits hop on fluffy feet.
They nibble leaves, making a mess,
Creating chaos, oh what a stress!

A bear tries climbing to grab a snack,
But tumbles back with a loud clack!
Berries splatter, a splashy fight,
Who knew fruit could bring such delight?

And when the harvest finally calls,
All critters rush, with wild brawls.
From cherries bright to grapes divine,
They feast and laugh, oh what a time!

A Canvas of Flavor

Fruit splashes bright on morning's plate,
With colors dancing, it's hard to wait.
Blueberries burst, while strawberries blush,
A giggling salad, oh what a rush!

The oranges roll, like they're in a race,
Lemons chuckle, making a face.
Bananas slip, almost in disguise,
With silly peels and wide-open eyes!

Kiwis in coats of fuzzy delight,
Prance 'round the bowl with all their might.
While cherries tease with their juicy pluck,
They jive and wiggle, oh aren't they luck?

At picnics, the fruit would start a band,
With berries drumming and apples so grand.
So grab a slice, don't be shy,
For fruity fun is worth a try!

Rustling Secrets

Whispers dance among the leaves,
As cheeky critters share their thieves.
A raccoon steals a peach so plump,
Then trips and lands with a funny thump!

Peaches giggle with juicy delight,
While plums plot mischief, giving a fright.
The winds carry tales, from branch to bough,
Of misfit fruits and how they endow!

A sly old fox peers through the green,
Smelling sweet nectar, oh what a scene!
But when he pounces, with a twirl and spin,
He lands in grapes, oh where to begin?

In secret shadows, laughter takes flight,
As fruits share jokes in the pale moonlight.
The night is young, with stories to rife,
In the rustling secrets of fruit's silly life!

Ripening Hues

Colors bloom in nature's booth,
With giggles ripe in every youth.
Yellow lemons with grins so wide,
A party of fruits on this crazy ride!

Apples blush in red's embrace,
While green grapes twirl with happy grace.
They pop and fizzle, a fruity spree,
As laughter bubbles in harmony!

The nectarines flaunt their glossy skin,
With quirky moves, they spin and spin.
Berries explode like confetti bright,
In this vibrant jamboree tonight!

And as the sun dips low in the sky,
The fruits unite with a joyful sigh.
Together they sing in harmonious hues,
A wondrous tale of ripening views!

Moments in the Meadow

In the meadow, sheep play tag,
But watch your step, or you'll snag!
A cow wears sunglasses, oh so sly,
While chickens gossip, oh my my!

A pig tries dancing, what a sight,
He twirls and squeals, with all his might!
The ducks, they quack, in perfect time,
With silly antics, rhythm and rhyme.

With butterflies that chase the breeze,
A bumblebee steals honey, if you please!
The farmer laughs, with hands on hips,
As cows start mooing, doing flips!

In this funny farm, joy is spread,
With every prank, a giggle fed!
So come along, just take a seat,
And join the fun, it's quite a treat!

Coral Blooms and Sunny Glades

In the glades, the flowers chat,
While daisies judge a passing cat.
The tulips gossip in bright hues,
Their petals flap like fancy shoes!

A squirrel juggles acorns with flair,
A raccoon shows off his wild hair.
The ladybugs hold a dance-off,
While a snail shimmies, ready to scoff!

The sunflowers peek from tall above,
Creating shadows — or is it love?
A bumblebee plays the DJ role,
While daisies dream of rock and roll.

With coral blooms, the laughter lands,
Nature's party, no need for plans!
Join in the fun, and swirl around,
In sunny glades, joy can be found!

Festival of Flavor

The festival starts with pies galore,
But watch out for the pies that soar!
A quirky chef flips ketchup high,
As tomatoes laugh and start to fly!

The pickles march in a parade,
While onions bring a zesty trade.
But when the garlic takes the stage,
All taste buds shout in pure outrage!

A pepper plays the maracas well,
And carrots join for a groovy spell.
While corn on the cob does a spin,
As popcorn bursts — let the fun begin!

So grab a dog, and dance in time,
With flavors blending, oh so prime!
The festival rolls on through the night,
Bringing laughter, food, and pure delight!

A Canvas of Colors

In colors bright, the earth does sing,
With splashes wild, like puppies spring!
Redbirds paint the sky with cheer,
While blues and greens all twirl near!

A rainbow wig on a grumpy bear,
Can make him giggle beyond compare!
With splatters from a dainty dove,
It feels like nature's fun-filled glove!

Butterflies wear crowns of thorns,
As squirrels complain about their horns.
A colorful mess, the trees declare,
With giggles hiding everywhere!

So hop along, with paints to share,
In this canvas, joy's the layer!
Nature's laughter fills the air,
As colors dance without a care!

Under the Boughs of Bliss

Under boughs where shadows play,
The squirrels plot their grand buffet.
With acorns tossed and laughter shared,
The trees look on, a bit impaired.

A robin sings a silly tune,
While bees burst forth, a buzzing boon.
They tumble 'round in pollen fights,
And flower crowns soon reach new heights.

Children giggle, running wide,
As fruits roll down the grassy slide.
A ripe tomato joins the chase,
The veggies giggle, what a race!

Under boughs with joy so pure,
A fruit punch stands, a sweet allure.
And all around, the laughter flows,
In this wild garden, anything goes!

Serene Harvests

In fields where mischief comes to bloom,
    The pumpkins plot a fruity gloom.
They whisper schemes beneath the sun,
    To trip the farmer just for fun.

As apples swing from branches high,
    They practice jokes, oh me, oh my!
A pear pipes up, "I can't believe,
    That orange thinks it can deceive!"

With baskets full, a comical sight,
    A hapless goat, he takes a bite.
He munches down on all that's round,
    And rolls away without a sound.

Meanwhile, the harvest cheers with glee,
    For every veggie, fruit, and pea.
In this serene and playful scene,
    Life's fruits unite in laughter's sheen!

The Dance of Tender Leaves

Leaves that twirl as breezes twine,
They flirt and prance in pairs divine.
With every gust, a playful tease,
Gathering gossip from the trees.

A acorn thumps upon the ground,
"Hey, leafy friends, you spin around!"
While mushrooms giggle down below,
The fertile earth delights the show.

A while turtle joins the dance,
Moving slow, it takes a chance.
With every shuffle, roots protrude,
As nature jigs, it's all good mood.

And in this ballet, light and spry,
The sunbeams laugh; they dance on high.
Underneath the frolic's weave,
Joy abounds, you best believe!

Nectar's Embrace

Bees and flowers, a sticky tale,
Buzzing dreams on a perfumed sail.
"Dance," they shout, and twirl with grace,
As nectar flows, it's quite the race!

A daisy laughs, "You can't catch me!"
As a bumblebee sips sweetly.
With wiggles, giggles, and a spin,
They paint the air, let joys begin.

Pollination, a comical flurry,
In this flower world, there's no worry.
Each blossom knows their charm's the key,
To win a heart, oh can't you see?

So raise a glass, let's clink and cheer,
For every pollinator near!
In nature's play, the fun expands,
As sweetness reigns in busy hands!

Sunlit Abundance

Beneath the sunny trees, we play,
With fruits so bright, we laugh away.
A pear fell down, oh what a sight,
We dodged it fast; it took a flight.

The apples grin, they tease and roll,
One lands on Uncle Bob's tall soul.
He trips and yells, 'These fruits are sly!'
We giggle loud; the birds all sigh.

Ripened Dreams

In dreams, I float on cherries sweet,
A silly dance with dancing feet.
The plums all wink, they whisper schemes,
To make us slip in fruity memes.

A grape went rogue, it made a dash,
Caught in a vine, oh what a clash!
We tumbled down in berry glee,
As laughter echoed, wild and free.

Joyful Harvests

The harvest day is here, let's cheer,
With baskets wide, we squeeze in cheer.
A cantaloupe shouts, 'Pick me too!'
But wait, it rolls—what's it to do?

We chase it round like playful kids,
As laughter slips from shy little lids.
The veggies chuckle, join the fun,
In garden games, we're never done.

Seasons of Delight

The seasons change, with fruits that pout,
They contort, twist, and twist about.
A squash complains, it feels so bare,
It dreams of days with sun and air.

The berries plot their sweet escape,
To find a world of fruity cape.
We giggle at the silly scene,
As every fruit strives to be seen.

Mirth Among the Fruits

In the grove where apples laugh,
Peaches dance on popsicle paths.
A pear in a tutu spins with glee,
While strawberries juggle under the tree.

Grapes are grinning, rolling as they roll,
Plums wear hats, what a silly stroll!
Cherries chuckle, causing a fuss,
As figs play leapfrog on top of us.

Lemons, they open a pickle jar,
Claiming that pickles are their cousin's star.
Bananas slip and slide away,
Yelling, "Catch me if you can, hooray!"

In this fruit parade, laughter sprouts,
Nature's giggles amongst the shouts.
Every bite brings a chuckle and cheer,
In this garden, fun is always near.

Glimmers of Grace

Oranges glow like lanterns bright,
Whispering secrets in the night.
With every peel comes a burst of cheer,
And kiwis giggle, "We're almost here!"

Berries roll in a merry chase,
As melons try their funny grace.
A lemon slips, oops, down it goes,
Landing in a patch of silly pose.

Raspberries complain, "Too red for me!"
While limes declare, "I'm the life of the tea!"
Avocados, smooth, just strut their stuff,
Claiming they're cool, but are they tough?

Fruit salads sing in harmony,
Dancing spoons in a bowl, so free.
Laughter bubbles with every tune,
In this garden, fun is out of tune.

Eternal Bloom

In a field where daisies wear hats,
Watermelons play poker with bats.
"Who's got the best seeds?" they cheerfully brawl,
As cucumbers witness this wild call.

Tulips shout, "We're the flower crown!"
While carrots sport socks and dance around.
The sunflowers stretch, reaching up high,
Tickled by breezes that dance in the sky.

Herbs make jokes in fragrances sweet,
Telling tales that make even bees tweet.
Lavenders laugh as they spill their pot,
Wishing for laughter and love in a lot.

In this garden, joy doesn't cease,
As blossoms spread warmth, a simple peace.
Each bloom a giggle, a tease of delight,
In every corner, fun takes flight.

The Tickle of Tenderness

A peach in a hammock sways with a grin,
Telling a pear, "Come join in the spin!"
Plums start a giggle about their soft skin,
While nectarines cheer, "Let the fun begin!"

Cherries dangle, trying to reach,
To tickle the lemons as they preach.
Oranges burst into a round of cheers,
Keeping time with the seasonal years.

Each fruit plays a role in this grand charade,
Making music in harmony, never afraid.
With laughter and puns hanging like vines,
The sweetness of joy in the world brightly shines.

In this patch, where whimsy blooms,
Even the wind hums with cheerful tunes.
All the fruits united in playful jest,
Creating a garden, joy truly blessed.

A Dance of Colors

Beneath the sun, the fruits do sway,
An apple twirls, a cheerful display.
Bananas giggle, they slip and slide,
While grapes hold hands in a fruity glide.

Lemons shout with zest, oh so bold,
A jolly crowd, a sight to behold.
Peaches drop in laughter, rolling fast,
Creating a mess, but who can be aghast?

Peppers play tag, a spicy affair,
Carrots burst giggles, floating in air.
A rainbow ruckus, a feast for the eyes,
Where nature's palette wears silly disguise.

Come join the frolic, leave woes behind,
In this realm of chuckles, delightfully blind.
With each shiny fruit, a punchline's near,
A dance of colors, where laughter's sincere.

A Tapestry of Fruits

In the garden, fruits weave a show,
Strawberries whisper secrets, you know.
Pineapples chuckle, spikes up so high,
While ripe mangoes wink, oh my oh my!

Melons float by like ships in a race,
Bouncing and rolling, they find their place.
A fruit salad band strikes up a tune,
With cherries and kiwis, they dance 'neath the moon.

Oranges giggle as they peel away,
Leaving zesty trails, come join the play!
Each flavor a note in this fruity blend,
A tapestry woven, where laughter won't end.

Together they frolic, a merry brigade,
Creating a joy, that'll never fade.
In this silly garden, we find our cheer,
A fruity fiesta, come dance, my dear!

Fields of Friendship

In fields where laughter springs forth loud,
Berries and nuts, they're meeting the crowd.
A tomato juggles, a sight to behold,
While corn on the cob boasts stories retold.

On sunny days, they gather in cheer,
Pumpkins roll over, spreading good cheer.
A beet prances by in a wobbly way,
While zucchinis leap, oh what a display!

A friendship of fruits, colorful core,
With watermelon smiles, who could ask for more?
Tomatoes play soccer, squashed in the mud,
In laughter and giggles, they dance in the flood.

Together they grow, in sun and in rain,
In fields of friendship, there's never a strain.
With every new harvest, a spark of delight,
In this merry patch, everything feels right.

Fruits of Togetherness

A berry brigade bounces, oh what a sight,
As fruits gather 'round, all merry and bright.
A pear sings a tune, with a comical flair,
While cherries do cartwheels, without a care.

Kiwi brings laughter, green fuzzy delight,
As limes throw confetti, a zesty invite.
With apples a-marching, in line like a team,
The orchard's a stage, living the dream.

Each fruit brings a story, a chuckle or two,
Pineapple's puns, oh they always break through.
In this bright gathering, no worries reside,
With laughter and fun always on the side.

Fruits of togetherness, a joyful embrace,
In the dance of flavors, we find our grace.
With each silly moment, we gather and grow,
In this wacky world, we steal the show!

Overhead Canopies

Beneath the trees, we play and leap,
A squirrel steals a snack, oh dear,
Chasing shadows, losing sleep,
The laughter echoes far and near.

The apples giggle in the sun,
While pears are plotting mischief, too,
We race around, we're on the run,
Who knew fruit could act like a crew?

The branches sway, we start to dance,
With every step, our troubles cease,
The bees hum loud, they take a chance,
To join our wild and sweet release.

A picnic spread, we munch and munch,
But watch out for that sneaky crow,
He's got a knack for a sneaky lunch,
And off he flies with our last dough!

Golden Hours in Bloom

Beneath the glow, we find our glee,
A butterfly wore stripes today,
We chase its dance, so wild and free,
While ants march by in a parade.

With lemonade and silly straws,
We giggle till our cheeks turn red,
The fruits debate their silly flaws,
And burst with laughter overhead.

We play a game, who can throw tight,
A peach up high without a splat,
It lands on Dad; what a delight!
A splash of juice, now he's a cat!

The sun dips low, it's time for treats,
We roast marshmallows, just a few,
While singing songs to dancing beats,
The perfect end; we bid adieu!

Fields of Joy

In fields of green, we skip and roll,
A tumble here, a hop, a spree,
With giggles lifting, pure as coal,
We chase the wind, we laugh with glee.

Dandelions puff their seed,
Like tiny parachutes on high,
We make a wish, oh yes indeed,
To fly away and touch the sky.

Bouncing balls and games galore,
The laughter echoes, loud and clear,
A frisbee flies, but what's in store?
It lands right in the chipmunk's beer!

As twilight wraps us in its arms,
We share our tales of silly pranks,
The stars will twinkle, draw us charms,
In fields of dreams, we leave our thanks!

Elysium in the Orchard

In a realm where laughter soars,
The fruit is ripe with endless grace,
Corny jokes and silly roars,
We skip around at a funny pace.

The trees hush tales, a breeze so sly,
A jumble of fruits, all in a chat,
An apple whispers, oh my, oh my,
"That pear just wore my favorite hat!"

Together we dig up the ground,
Hunting for treasures, sticky hands,
We find a shoe, it's quite profound,
What were they doing in the sands?

As evening falls with a soft embrace,
We sit with smiles all around,
In this place of love and grace,
The fruit and laughter will astound!

Savoring Sunshine

In the garden where laughter blooms,
Fruit hangs low, cheering up our rooms.
Baboons in hats play peek-a-boo,
Claiming each apple, just for their crew.

Sun beams down like a cheeky friend,
Tickling the vines that twist and bend.
Lemons are juggling, their citrusy flair,
Oranges roll by, unaware of the dare.

A squirrel on stilts prances with grace,
Stealing a peach, oh what a chase!
The berries in giggles start to unite,
Planning a party, oh what a sight!

Laughter echoes through every green lane,
As nature's clowns dance in the rain.
We sip on nectar, our worries adrift,
Thanking the sun for this fruity gift.

Roots of Radiance

Under leaves where shadows play,
Rooted jokes sprout every day.
A carrot cracks wise about a pie,
While cabbages whisper a secret sly.

Beets wear glasses, looking quite spry,
Composing bad puns as the time flies by.
The radishes roll with laughter so loud,
While lettuce gets lost in a leafy crowd.

A potato sings the blues with flair,
Telling tales of starch without a care.
The pumpkins giggle, their guts all aglow,
Sharing secrets of what they might grow.

With roots intertwined, in joyful mirth,
They celebrate life, the dirt, and its worth.
A funny fest blooms beneath the sun,
Where every veggie knows it's all in good fun.

Melodies Among the Melons

In a patch where watermelons jive,
A cantaloupe hums, feeling alive.
They dance under stars, quite out of tune,
Sipping sweet nectar, swaying till noon.

Honeydews winking and sharing a laugh,
Slicing up stories, each melon's own half.
Laughter ricochets off the vines so bright,
As they juggle seeds in pure delight.

The squashes complain they're left out of plays,
But join in the fun, finding funny ways.
A watermelon yodels with seed-spitting might,
While the others cheer, "What a glorious sight!"

In this fruity fiesta, where melodies swell,
They giggle and wiggle, no need to compel.
Each song bubbles up with a sweet, silly punch,
In this garden of laughter, a festive brunch!

Essence of Elation

Apples don tutus, ready to twirl,
While lemons do flips in a dizzy swirl.
Grapes groan with joy in a bunch so grand,
Crafting wild tales with a fruity band.

The cherries declare a dance-off spree,
While the figs laugh, "Just wait, you'll see!"
Bananas slip in and steal the show,
Joking around, as the audience glows.

Pineapples sport shades, looking so cool,
They slide through the orchard like it's a pool.
Peaches pop jokes, ripe and so sweet,
Establishing laughter as their main treat.

With every punchline that bursts from their core,
The fruits bring joy, and we all want more.
In this vibrant space where giggles abound,
Elation sings sweetly, all around!

Cradled by Green

In a sea of apples, I sway and spin,
Worms are my friends, they always grin.
Chasing the bees that tickle my nose,
Silly little critters, they come with their pose.

Underneath branches, I dance with glee,
Talking to pumpkins and ants for tea.
Every plump peach has a story to share,
Fruit salad laughter fills the sweet air.

Carrots throw parties and cabbages sing,
A merry-go-round made of everything!
Lettuce plays tag while radishes sneak,
Nature's own circus, oh what a week!

Life in the greens is a whimsical play,
Where every leaf dances, come join the fray.
Giggles and chuckles just might make you stay,
In this garden of laughter, we frolic all day!

Raindrops and Radiance

Raindrops are plucking the strings of the leaves,
Making a melody that giggles and weaves.
Cherries are laughing, their cheeks are so bright,
Splashing in puddles, oh what a sight!

Drizzles of joy are tumbling down,
Dancing with daisies while wearing a crown.
Sunshine peeks through with a mischievous wink,
Telling the raindrops, 'Come on, let's drink!'

Marigolds merry, in skirts of pure gold,
Whisper sweet secrets that never grow old.
A fruit punch parade happens nearby,
Juggling with lemons while blueberries fly.

Every splash, every giggle, a moment divine,
Each droplet's a sparkle, a sip of sunshine.
Nature conspired for this playful spree,
Join in the chorus of happy decree!

Gathered Joy

Baskets of laughter, I gather them fast,
Fruits doing cartwheels, what a bold cast!
Strawberries giggle, while blueberries leap,
Mangoes and melons in a fruity heap.

Walnuts are chuckling, they spill and they roll,
Coconuts bouncing like they're on a stroll.
Bananas start waltzing, they slip and they slide,
With a pink pom-pom, they dance side by side.

Tossing the berries into a grand mix,
Fruits playing charades in their funny tricks.
Gathering joy feels like a big game,
In the bright sun, we dance with no shame.

Whoopee pies calling, 'Come take a chance!',
Every sweet treat joins in our dance.
In the garden of giggles, we feast like kings,
With baskets of joy, oh see what it brings!

Heartfelt Harvest

This harvest is funny, full of delight,
Carrots are chuckling, what a silly sight!
Each veggie's a character, wearing a grin,
Dancing together, they pull us right in.

Tomatoes are teasing, 'We are ripe and red!',
Zucchini shares jokes from his leafy bed.
Peppers are teasing in bright shades of green,
Flavors competition, a comical scene.

Aren't beets just the cutest, all round and plump?
They wiggle and giggle; they really do jump!
Onions are crying, but don't shed a tear,
Just laugh with the harvest, the fun's really here!

With hearts full of joy, let's dance and sing,
Celebrate all that each plant can bring.
In this quirky farm where the smiles align,
Life's sweetest harvest is funny and fine!

www.ingramcontent.com/pod-product-compliance
Lightning Source LLC
Chambersburg PA
CBHW062113280426
43661CB00086B/584